Contents

KV-241-400

Pathfinder 28

A CILT series for language teachers

Making effective use of the dictionary

Gwen Berwick and Phil Horsfall

Other titles in the PATHFINDER series:

Being creative (Barry Jones)

Bridging the gap: GCSE to 'A' level (John Thorogood and Lid King)

Communication re-activated: teaching pupils with learning difficulties
    (Bernardette Holmes)

Continuous assessment and recording (John Thorogood)

Creative use of texts (Bernard Kavanagh and Lynne Upton)

Departmental planning and schemes of work (Clive Hurren)

Developing skills for independent reading (Iain Mitchell and Ann Swarbrick)

Differentiation (Anne Convery and Do Coyle)

Drama in the languages classroom (Judith Hamilton and Anne McLeod)

Exploring otherness — an approach to cultural awareness (Barry Jones)

Fair enough? Equal opportunities and modern languages (Vee Harris)

Grammar matters (Susan Halliwell)

Improve your image: the effective use of the OHP (Daniel Tierney and Fay Humphreys)

Keeping on target (Bernardette Holmes)

Listening in a foreign language — a skill we take for granted? (Karen Turner)

New contexts for modern language learning (Kim Brown and Margot Brown)

Nightshift — ideas and strategies for homework (David Buckland and Mike Short)

Not bothered? Motivating reluctant learners in Key Stage 4 (Jenifer Alison)

On target — teaching in the target language (Susan Halliwell and Barry Jones)

Reading for pleasure in a foreign language (Ann Swarbrick)

With a song in my scheme of work (Steven Fawkes)

Yes — but will they behave? Managing the interactive classroom (Susan Halliwell)

First published 1996
Copyright © 1996 Centre for Information on Language Teaching and Research
ISBN 1 874016 60 7

Cover by Logos Design
Printed in Great Britain by Oakdale Printing Co Ltd

Published by the Centre for Information on Language Teaching and Research,
20 Bedfordbury, Covent Garden, London WC2N 4LB.

Introduction

Although the dictionary has always been an indispensable tool for university language students and those who work with modern languages, it hardly ever used to be mentioned in school textbooks. Recently, however, it has come to be recognised as a valuable tool for school pupils and its use is now actively promoted.

WHY ARE DICTIONARY SKILLS IMPORTANT?

Curriculum and exam syllabus designers now acknowledge the importance of reference materials in various aspects of language learning and use:

Communication and authenticity

Authenticity has always been one of the key concepts of communicative language teaching. Authentic texts are produced for a native speaker audience in the real world, and thus often contain vocabulary and structures not known to a non-native speaker. Use of such texts helps to accustom learners to dealing with the kinds of language they will meet in real situations. If we are to prepare our pupils to use the foreign language for study, work and leisure, we must help them to develop the skills and judgement to use tools such as reference materials appropriately.

Autonomy

Pupils who can use reference materials with confidence are well on their way to becoming much more independent learners. They have greater control over their own learning, and are not so dependent on the teacher. This helps to engender greater motivation and self-esteem. At the same time, it can help to free the teacher from being a 'walking dictionary' to spend time with pupils more productively.

Differentiation

A dictionary can be used to help with problems at a range of levels, from checking spelling to finding a word in the target language. More able pupils in a class will make greater use of the dictionary, freeing the teacher to spend time with others.

Transferable skills

Dictionary skills developed in the study of one language can be used not only in studying and using other languages, but can also help in the use of other reference materials, such as mother tongue dictionaries, encyclopaedias, grammar reference books and telephone directories.

Dictionary skills are obviously important. However, in untrained hands, a dictionary can be more of a hindrance than a help, as shown by these 'dictionary bloomers', taken from the Strathclyde Regional Council Dictionary Skills pack!

> *tu bidon visite . . .*
> *je pièce billard*
> *je ne suis pas puits*
> *je scie le Ifile Tuor*
> *à pied le chien*
> *pers pron prep entrer en scène l'Ecosse*
> *j'utilisais discuter avec ma mère*
> *je vais à France du 18 caisse 25 juillet*

Pupils need to **learn** how to a use a dictionary efficiently and effectively. The aim of this Pathfinder is to help you to help your pupils to do just that.

1. Using a dictionary

 FIRST DICTIONARY SKILLS FOR WORD LISTS

The ideal starting point for learning dictionary skills is the glossary at the back of your coursebook. There are also available simplified vocabulary books for younger pupils, some of which use colour-coding to reinforce such concepts as gender.

THE FL ALPHABET AND ACCENTS

Before any language learner can begin to use any reference materials, he or she must be familiar with the letters of the target language. At the same time, a familiarisation with the accents in the target language is important for distinguishing between similar words, e.g. *sucre* and *sucré,* as well as for pronunciation and, in languages like Spanish, stress.

Useful activities include:

▶ Write on the board or OHP five familiar words from the topic being studied, with their accents missing. Ask pupils to look them up in the glossary of their textbook and copy them out with the accents.

▶ For a language with a different script, you could transliterate the names of famous people into the script, for pupils to decode. They could then make up some others for their classmates.

ALPHABETICAL ORDER

The next stage is to begin familiarity with alphabetical order. Clearly, this is much easier for languages using the Roman alphabet, but nothing should be taken for granted. Many pupils can recite the whole alphabet from the start, but if asked in a vacuum whether the letter *r* comes before or after the letter *p,* they would be flummoxed for a while. Pupils also need to know how particular features of the language are dealt with in the dictionary. In Spanish, for example, words beginning *ll* have a separate section. Pupils need to know whether or not accents affect alphabetical order in the language they are learning.

This is a good opportunity to revise or introduce the pronunciation of the alphabet in the target language as well, and it is worth asking the class if they can think of other times, apart from when looking up words in a dictionary, that this familiarity with the alphabet might help (e.g. telephone directory, street map index).

Activities which help with familiarising pupils with the alphabet might include:

- Filling in missing letters in a sequence, e.g. 'opq _'; '_stu'; 'e _ g'.
- Rearranging sequential and non-sequential sets of letters alphabetically, e.g. 'lknm'; 'lfp'.
- Rearranging letters alphabetically to form a word in the target language, e.g. 'ojibu' gives the French word *bijou*.
- Giving target language words in a simple code (e.g. pupils need to replace each letter by the letter just before it in the alphabet, e.g. 'Ivoe' = *Hund*).

SELECTING THE CORRECT MEANING

Some entries in a word list may have more than one translation, and pupils should learn to think about which one fits best into the given context. At this early stage, this is best done as a class, with close guidance from the teacher.

Knowing when not to look up a word

One of the most important skills is knowing when **not** to look up a word, and alternative strategies to use. You can encourage your pupils from the start to think about the probable meaning in the given context, to use clues such as pictures, and to guess cognates. Strategies for more advanced pupils are outlined in Chapter 3.

Features of word lists in your coursebook

Coursebooks adopt varying conventions for their glossary: some have standard dictionary features, e.g. *maison (nf)*, while others are simpler, e.g. *une maison*. You need to familiarise your students with the particular format of the coursebook you use.

 ## USING A BILINGUAL DICTIONARY

As they graduate from glossaries to using a bilingual dictionary, there are a number of features with which pupils need to become familiar in order to use it effectively. Even though they may know how to use an English-English dictionary, and many of the skills are clearly transferable, using a bilingual dictionary involves additional particular skills. Some features vary slightly from dictionary to dictionary, so you may need to give help to individuals with their own dictionary as well as explaining the features of the one you use in class.

FINDING A WORD IN THE DICTIONARY

Firstly, pupils need to learn how they can quickly find the word they are looking for:

Structure and layout

Pupils need to know that the dictionary is arranged in two halves: Target Language–English and English–Target Language.

One way to begin is to direct pupils' attention to the headwords at the top of the page and help them to work out for themselves how using these will speed up their search. The exact system used varies from dictionary to dictionary. Some give the first and last headwords on each page of a spread, others give only the first headword on each page of a spread, while others give only the first and last headwords of the spread.

Activities to practise using these words could include the following:

- ▶ Pupils say whether or not they would expect to find particular words on given pages. For example, when looking up words during the topic of pets, would pupils expect to find *Hund* on the page headed *Huhn-Hypothek*?
- ▶ Pupils find out how many pages there are between two such headwords, for example *beater* and *brown*.
- ▶ Give pupils a list of key words from the topic your are working on. They look them up and note down the headword(s) at the top of the corresponding pages.
- ▶ Give pupils a list of topic-related headwords which are not found at the top of the page. They race to find them and note down the page number.

Encourage your pupils to explore the dictionary further and become more familiar with its features and specific characteristics of the target language. For example:

- ▶ Pupils have to find the pages with particular features, such as a regular declension or verb paradigms; common abbreviations; phrases for beginning and ending letters.

▷ Pupils have to predict whether certain sections of the dictionary will be longer or shorter than others, then look them up to check. For example, pupils could compare the lengths of the sections for the letters *C* and *K* in French, the number of pages for the letter *Z* in German and English. This activity also helps to extend pupils' awareness of the character of the target language.

Headwords

Understanding the role and function of headwords, other than those at the top of the page, is a key skill, although it is not necessary for pupils to know the technical term 'headword'. Many words which pupils will want to look up will be headwords in their own right, e.g. *I've eaten my **dinner**.* A common problem, however, is when pupils try to look up words which are not headwords, e.g. *I've **eaten** my dinner.* They need to understand how headwords operate and how they are marked out in their dictionary (for example, are they bold or in colour?). More able pupils could be encouraged to work out for themselves the nature of headwords.

For some languages, set phrases, compound words and separable verbs may cause problems. Pupils will need to be familiar with the conventions of their dictionary and will need lots of practice in identifying the relevant headword.

You may find the following activities useful:

▷ Give pupils a list containing some words which are headwords in their own right, such as infinitives and uninflected adjectives, and others which are not headwords, such as parts of a verb paradigm or inflected nouns. The pupils look them up and note them down under two headings: *headwords/not headwords*. You could help them to draw conclusions about what headwords are.
▷ Give pupils a list of words to do with the topic you are dealing with. Ask them to predict which will be headwords in their own right and which will not.
▷ Once you have established the nature of headwords, give pupils a list of words which are not in headword form. They have to write down what they think the headword will be, then check their predictions in the dictionary.
▷ Give pupils a number of short sentences containing compound words or separable verbs, for example, from the topic of 'daily routine': *Helga **steht** um sieben Uhr **auf**.* Pupils have to identify the correct headword.

It might also be of interest to discuss with your pupils the limitations of various dictionaries in terms of their size, scope, age, etc.

► Give groups of pupils a list of words. Each group works with one particular dictionary and tries to find the words on the list. The groups report back on how many and which of the words they have found. You could discuss with the class why certain words have not been found in some or any dictionaries (e.g. the word was too technical, not common, slang, too recent).

UNDERSTANDING THE DICTIONARY ENTRY

Once found, the complexity of a dictionary entry can be baffling to the untrained eye! However, pupils can soon learn to use the features they need to help them select the most appropriate translation from those given.

Grammatical information

Pupils should understand the usefulness of abbreviations denoting grammatical information such as parts of speech, feminine and plural variations, or what case a particular verb takes. These abbreviations can help to confirm that the correct word has been selected, as well as being important in ensuring that the word is used correctly. If pupils do not understand the purpose of these abbreviations, there is a real danger that they will mistake them for part of the translation!

Most abbreviations regarding parts of speech are straightforward. More complex ones, such as *vt* and *vi*, probably need not be explained: all most pupils need to know is that the word is a verb. Able pupils could be asked to try to work out the meanings of the abbreviations for themselves, given a selection of appropriate dictionary entries.

The type of practice you give will depend on the age and ability of your pupils and the features of the particular language. For example:

► Pupils look up a list of key nouns from the topic you are studying (given in English or the target language). They note whether they are masculine, feminine or neuter in the target language.
► Pupils look up a list of nouns in the target language and note how gender changes meaning. They could draw pictures or write sentences to illustrate them.

Der Leiter kauft eine Leiter.

La poêle est sur le poêle.

(Horsfall, *Dictionary skills French and German*, LCP)

- Give pupils a varied selection of target language words from your current topic. They look them up and note down the parts of speech.
- Pupils are given a word in English, such as 'race', which can be a noun or a verb. They have to find the word which corresponds to its meaning as a noun.
- Pupils have to find out whether particular verbs are followed by *à* or *de* in French, or the cases taken by particular prepositions in German or Russian.
- Give pupils a list of imperfective verbs in Russian. They note down the corresponding perfective forms.

Symbols and conventions

Where possible, encourage pupils to work out for themselves the symbols and conventions and the reasons behind them. Some common ones include:

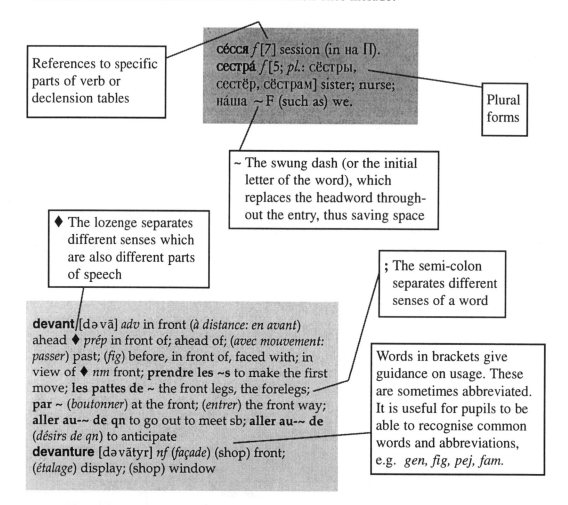

References to specific parts of verb or declension tables

сéсся *f* [7] session (in на П).
сестрá *f* [5; *pl.*: сёстры, сестёр, сёстрам] sister; nurse; нáша ~ F (such as) we.

Plural forms

~ The swung dash (or the initial letter of the word), which replaces the headword throughout the entry, thus saving space

♦ The lozenge separates different senses which are also different parts of speech

; The semi-colon separates different senses of a word

devant [də vɑ̃] *adv* in front (*à distance: en avant*) ahead ♦ *prép* in front of; ahead of; (*avec mouvement: passer*) past; (*fig*) before, in front of, faced with; in view of ♦ *nm* front; **prendre les ~s** to make the first move; **les pattes de ~** the front legs, the forelegs; **par ~** (*boutonner*) at the front; (*entrer*) the front way; **aller au-~ de qn** to go out to meet sb; **aller au-~ de** (*désirs de qn*) to anticipate
devanture [də vɑ̃tyr] *nf* (*façade*) (shop) front; (*étalage*) display; (shop) window

Words in brackets give guidance on usage. These are sometimes abbreviated. It is useful for pupils to be able to recognise common words and abbreviations, e.g. *gen, fig, pej, fam.*

You could try activities along the following lines:

▶ Pupils look up the references for given words in English or the target language and note down how many different meanings there are.

▶ Pupils have to find specific meanings, e.g. what does *accalappiare* mean when used figuratively?

Pronunciation guides

Many dictionaries give phonetic transcriptions or their equivalent. Pupils should know what these are, so they don't mistake them for a translation (it has been known!). Reassure them that they do not need to learn all the transcriptions, but should know where to look them up if necessary. Usually, they will only need to check part of the pronunciation.

Pupils should also understand indications of which syllables are stressed, where this is given.

The following activities might be useful:

▶ Give pupils learning Russian a list of words. They race to look them up and add stress marks over the appropriate syllables.

▶ Pupils learning Spanish could be given a list of words with no acute accents to show stress. They try to predict where the stress falls, then check their answers with the dictionary.

▶ Pupils learning French look up the following words: *impossible; inattentif; intelligent; incendie; imaginer; imitation; information; intéressant.* They note how the initial *i* is pronounced in each case. They can then be invited to formulate a general rule, based on their evidence. How many other words can they find to support their theory? Can they find any words which do not fit the pattern?

You could devise an activity such as the following, to draw together whichever of the above features you wish to practise with your class.

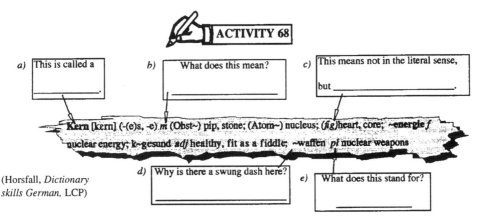

ACTIVITY 68

a) This is called a _____.

b) What does this mean? _____

c) This means not in the literal sense, but _____.

Kern [kern] (-(e)s, -e) *m* (Obst~) pip, stone; (Atom~) nucleus; (*fig*)heart, core; ~energie *f* nuclear energy; k~gesund *adj* healthy, fit as a fiddle; ~waffen *pl* nuclear weapons

d) Why is there a swung dash here? _____

e) What does this stand for? _____

(Horsfall, *Dictionary skills German*, LCP)

9

EFFECTIVE USE OF THE DICTIONARY ENTRY

As well as using their knowledge of the features outlined above to help them select the correct word, pupils should learn other important strategies:

Using the word correctly

It is important that pupils are aware that they often cannot just write down the word as they find it. It may need to be adapted to the specific context, for example a verb might need to be used in a form other than the infinitive.

You could work through some examples with pupils, then give them more to do on their own, for example:

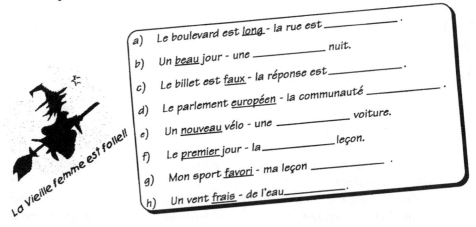

a) Le boulevard est <u>long</u> - la rue est _____ .

b) Un <u>beau</u> jour - une _____ nuit.

c) Le billet est <u>faux</u> - la réponse est _____ .

d) Le parlement <u>européen</u> - la communauté _____ .

e) Un <u>nouveau</u> vélo - une _____ voiture.

f) Le <u>premier</u> jour - la _____ leçon.

g) Mon sport <u>favori</u> - ma leçon _____ .

h) Un vent <u>frais</u> - de l'eau_____ .

La vieille femme est folle!!

(Horsfall, *Dictionary skills French,* LCP)

Checking with the context

When looking up a word, pupils should learn always to check that the translation they have selected fits the given context.

▶ Pupils look up the references for given words in English or the target language and note down how many different parts of speech there can be, e.g. *fly* can be a noun or a verb.
▶ Pupils have to choose which of two or more senses best fits a given context. E.g. *Ce prisonnier a volé de l'argent. (voler: to fly; to steal)*

- Give pupils sentences in the target language and equivalent sentences in English with gaps. Each gap has two alternative words in English. The pupils have to say which one fits the context. E.g. *Ce prisonnier a volé de l'argent. This prisoner _____ some money. (voler: to fly; to steal)*
- Pupils read sentences in which the wrong meaning of a word has been selected. They must find the correct meaning, e.g.
  *J'ai volé de Londres à Paris. I **stole** from London to Paris.*
  *My bag is very light. Mi bolsa es muy **luz**.*

Cross-referencing

When using a dictionary to find the appropriate target language translation of an English word, pupils must learn how to ensure they have selected the right word. They can start by using information regarding usage, as described on p10. However, there might still be more than one word to choose from. In this case, pupils need to get into the habit of looking up these words in the other half of the dictionary, to find which is most appropriate. This is where a monolingual dictionary may be particularly useful for more advanced pupils, as it gives much more detailed information and examples regarding usage.

- Provide English sentences related to the topic you are studying. Each sentence has one word underlined. Pupils have to look up the underlined word and find the word in the target language which best fits, for example: *My bag is very **light**.*

OTHER IMPORTANT USES OF THE DICTIONARY

Pupils should also learn that they can use their dictionary for purposes other than translating words. Some of these have been mentioned already, e.g. parts of speech, pronunciation. Some pupils might be able to suggest other uses of the dictionary. These could include:

- checking spellings;
- grammar reference, such as gender, alternative forms (e.g. *vendeur/vendeuse*), variations of adjectives (e.g. feminine, plural), verb aspect;
- declension and conjugation tables;
- proper nouns.

You could make sure your pupils know how such information is presented in the dictionary they use by using activities such as the following:

- It is important that pupils learn to read their own work critically to correct their mistakes. Give them sentences which contain words from the topic which are commonly misspelt. These words are underlined. Pupils have to use the dictionary to correct the spelling, e.g. *Ich interessiere mich für Musik.*
- Pupils have to use the dictionary to find irregular plurals, e.g. *un cheval, deux* _____; *un sac à dos, deux* _____; *un mes, dos* _____

USING A MONOLINGUAL DICTIONARY

WHICH TO USE: A BILINGUAL OR A MONOLINGUAL DICTIONARY?

Bilingual dictionaries are sometimes thought of as inferior to monolingual dictionaries, especially for advanced learners, and may seem to fit uneasily with methodology which encourages maximum use of the target language. However, both types of dictionary have advantages and disadvantages arising from differences in their nature and purpose.

A bilingual dictionary provides information required by non-native speakers of one of the languages, for whom it has been specifically designed. It gives direct translations and grammatical information to help users understand and manipulate words in the target language. Its main advantage over a monolingual dictionary is for productive purposes, when a specific word is not known in the target language. Users with limited knowledge of that language will find the bilingual dictionary more useful for comprehension as well: the monolingual paraphrase or definition may well be too difficult to understand. A good bilingual dictionary will contain other features useful to non-native speakers, such as verb tables.

For the more advanced learner a monolingual dictionary may have the following advantages:

- It involves a more direct engagement with the target language itself, rather than through the intermediary of translation into English.
- It encourages the learner to look beyond a simplistic one-to-one relationship between words in the two languages.
- It gives more information about the target language because it is aimed principally at native speakers of the language and therefore gives explanations and synonyms of words as well as information about usage and style. Obviously, it has more space than a bilingual dictionary of the same size, which must deal with sets of words from two languages, and can therefore give more examples of the word in a range of contexts. This increased understanding of the subtleties of usage is clearly of more value in productive use of the language than in receptive use.

- Some monolingual dictionaries are combined in the same volume with an encyclopaedia, which is useful for cultural awareness.

At the same time, even at an advanced level, however much useful information an entry in a monolingual dictionary might have, if a student does not know the right word to look up, this information will remain hidden away. The two types of dictionary can be used effectively to complement each other. For example, a bilingual dictionary can be used to identify possible appropriate translations of an English word. These words can then be cross checked in a monolingual dictionary, for confirmation that they are appropriate and for greater understanding of their usage.

LEARNING TO USE A MONOLINGUAL DICTIONARY

Pupils need to be able to judge when to use both types of dictionary appropriately, as outlined above.

They need to understand the conventions of the monolingual dictionary that they are using in the same way as they did for the bilingual dictionary. You could look at specific entries together and encourage your pupils to work out as much as they can, based on their knowledge and experience of a bilingual dictionary.

You could start with simple activities based on ones suggested for the bilingual dictionary, such as looking up words to find out specific information, e.g. part of speech, related preposition or case. You could then move on to more subtle aspects of usage, such as whether a particular word can be used in a given context.

DICTIONARY SKILLS AND THE TARGET LANGUAGE

There is some debate regarding whether the teaching of technical dictionary skills should be carried out in the target language or in English. It is generally agreed that it is desirable to maximise appropriate use of the target language in class. However, this is one situation where you might feel that it would be more appropriate to use English at times, since it would be absurd if the teacher's explanation were more complex than the pupils could possibly comprehend. How much of this explanation you attempt in the target language will obviously depend on the nature of the specific skill being explained and on the level and ability of the pupils. This may also apply to the exploitation activities which follow the explanation, although it is easier to devise an activity in the target language to practise a skill which has already been explained in English.

- Very simple principles could be explained to younger pupils in the target language, with use of mime, practical demonstration and example e.g. *'Le dictionnaire a deux sections: Français-Anglais* (open dictionary and show to class) *et Anglais-Français.'*
- Equally, you could display enlarged copies of a dictionary entry on the OHP, and then indicate certain features and explain them in the target language, e.g.
  Bild (-er) <— *Das hier ist die Pluralform, also ein Bild, aber zwei Bilder.*
- However, more complex features such as the use of the swung dash and skills such as effective use of the dictionary entry might be too difficult for pupils to follow in the target language. Clearly, you must use your discretion as to what is appropriate for your class.
- However the skill has been explained, many follow-up activities are possible in the target language. For example:

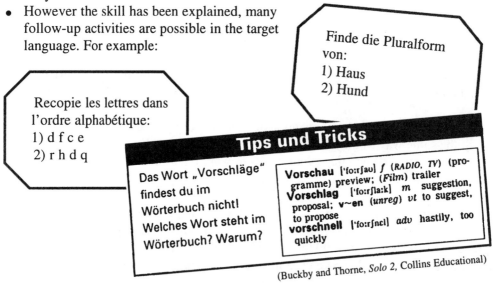

Finde die Pluralform von:
1) Haus
2) Hund

Recopie les lettres dans l'ordre alphabétique:
1) d f c e
2) r h d q

Tips und Tricks

Das Wort „Vorschläge" findest du im Wörterbuch nicht! Welches Wort steht im Wörterbuch? Warum?

Vorschau ['foːrʃau] *f* (RADIO, TV) (programme) preview; (Film) trailer
Vorschlag ['foːrʃlaːk] *m* suggestion, proposal; v~en (unreg) *vt* to suggest, to propose
vorschnell ['foːrʃnɛl] *adv* hastily, too quickly

(Buckby and Thorne, *Solo 2*, Collins Educational)

Many activities for developing dictionary skills could be given on worksheets, and thus would be ideal for homework. This would be particularly useful where pupils did not have their own copy of a coursebook, making it impossible to set homework from that. It should be borne in mind, however, that library provision would have to be made to accommodate those pupils who did not have their own dictionary.

DICTIONARY GAMES

Learning how to use a bilingual dictionary, with all its grammatical terms and abbreviations, is no different from learning a foreign language itself, in that it can be fun if the approach is enlivened with games to encourage the learners and to sustain their interest. Games also mean that the learners are more likely to want to take part, since there is a more immediate purpose to the activity beyond the practice of a dictionary skill - the challenge of the game subsumes the challenge of the dictionary skill. Games can allow pupils to work in pairs or groups to practise a dictionary skill that will ultimately be used almost exclusively in an individual context. The following will give a flavour of the kinds of games that pupils can use to practise dictionary skills, and you will certainly come up with many variations on these themes and additional ideas.

- ▶ To speed up finding a word, pupils work in pairs and you write up on the board some words in the target language and some English words. Pupils take it in turns to open the dictionary first time as near to the word as possible. You then say the correct page number of the given word, and pupils compare (with a calculator if necessary!) to see who was the fewest pages from the right one.

- ▶ A similar variation is simply 'Who's quickest?'. Pupils work in groups. One pupil chooses a word in English or the target language and challenges the others to find it in the dictionary. The first person to find and show the word sets the next challenge.

- ▶ Advanced pupils might enjoy playing *Scrabble* in the target language.

- ▶ You could make up variations on crosswords, word searches, acrostics and games like *Call My Bluff* or *Blankety Blank,* or '*mots cassés*', e.g.

MOTS CASSÉS

There are twelve French words hidden in the grid below. Each word is made up of five letters but has been split into two parts.
Find the French words. Each group of letters can only be used once.
Use your dictionary to help you.

fer	lge	at	ta	fou	re
can	ma	le	pr	su	rin
ise	bac	cre	ég	ine	por
te	ach	me	be	out	ot

(Tayside Regional Council, *Dictionary skills in the French class*)

▶ Pupils have to predict which word out of a group of four does **not** exist in the target language, based on their knowledge of vocabulary and typical features of the language, and use the dictionary to check, e.g.

Er fährt mit . . .   *dem Fahrrad*
            der Straßenbahn
            der Plenkheit
            dem Luftkissenfahrzeug

▶ Invent a word ladder like the following:

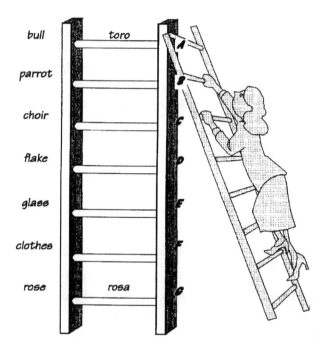

bull	toro
parrot	
choir	
flake	
glass	
clothes	
rose	rosa

(Evans, *Dictionary skills Spanish*, LCP)

▶ You could invent a word maze like the following, or a simplified version. Once you have a template, you can use it for different topic areas and also give pupils their own blank copy to invent a puzzle for their partner.

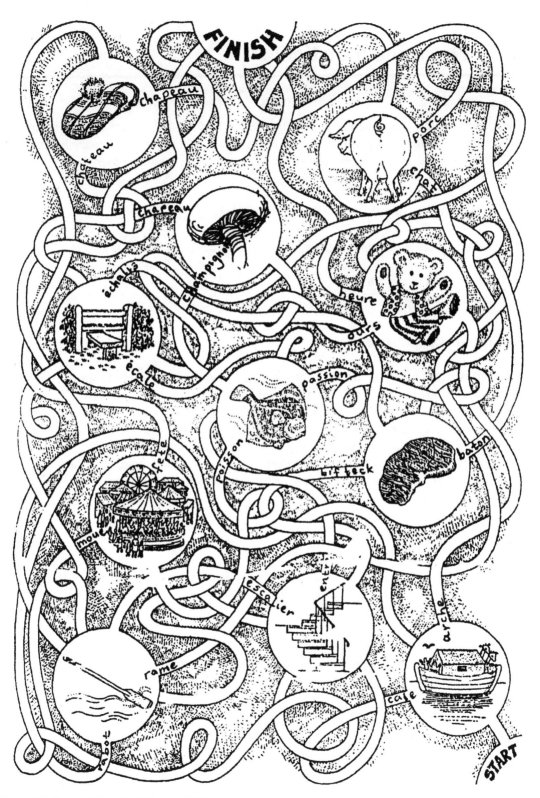

2.   Not using a dictionary

Used appropriately, the dictionary is an invaluable tool for learners of a foreign language. However, the ability to know when and how to avoid using a dictionary helps to make the learner a more independent, capable and confident language user.

 ## REASONS FOR NOT USING THE DICTIONARY

It is useful to discuss with pupils the limitations of a dictionary in terms of:

- knowing a language; and
- real life situations.

'KNOWING' A LANGUAGE

You could discuss with your pupils what it means to **know,** or to be able to speak another language. Knowing a language means being able to produce and understand that language. It involves knowledge and understanding of words and how they are used. The competent language user needs to have language available for instant recognition, recall and use, as opposed to just knowing where to find out about it. An analogy could be drawn with driving a car: the driver has to know how to brake and change gear and must recognise and understand road signs. Just being able to refer to the manual and the highway code is clearly not enough in practice!

REAL-LIFE PRACTICALITY

Discuss with your pupils real life situations in which language use requires instantly available knowledge. One possible activity is as follows:

▶ Give pupils a list of situations, e.g.
   While staying at your penfriend's house:
   - Understanding what your penfriend's parents are saying to you.
   - Having a conversation with your penfriend.
   - Asking to borrow something.

At your own home:
- Reading a letter from your penfriend.
- Writing to a tourist office to ask for information.
- Reading a magazine sent by your penfriend.
- Listening to a radio programme in the foreign language.

When on holiday abroad:
- Understanding a tannoy announcement at the railway station.
- Understanding a sign at the ticket office of a theme park.
- Making a complaint about your hotel room.

Pupils have to say in which of these situations they might be able to use a dictionary for help, and in which it would not really be practical, and if not, why not. Write up these reasons on the board or OHP.

Reasons are likely to include:
- Lack of time (e.g. particularly when listening and speaking, unless, for speaking, you have time in advance to prepare and check a word you **know** you will need).
- When listening, it is difficult to look up a word you haven't understood or recognised, because you might not know how to spell it. This is particularly true for languages like French, where spelling is not all phonetic.
- It is impractical to carry a dictionary around.
- Even the most sympathetic native speaker will lose patience if your every utterance is punctuated by dictionary use.

PRACTICALITIES IN CLASS

Discuss with your pupils the implications of the above for dictionary use in the classroom, in each of the four skill areas. Possible activities include:

- ▶ Pupils say which of the reasons they identified above apply to the different kinds of work they do in class.
- ▶ They then add other reasons (e.g. they may have to share dictionaries in class).
- ▶ Look at the problems particular to each skill area.

ACCURACY

It is also important to point out that by sticking to already known language as far as possible when speaking and writing, pupils will ensure greater accuracy in their work. This might be particularly important in a given situation, such as in the exam.

In the light of the above, it is important to stress to pupils the need to learn vocabulary. Some suggestions for this are given in Chapter 4.

 ## STRATEGIES TO USE

Pupils can learn useful strategies to help them avoid using the dictionary.

Reading and listening:

- Do I really need to know the meaning?
- Can I work out the meaning from the context, using my common sense?
- Is the word similar to an English word or one I know in another language? (Remember that some words are 'false friends': always check the context.)
- Do the titles and pictures help me to understand?
- Does the word follow a pattern I've met before? E.g. I know *revenir* and *prendre*, so I can work out *reprendre*.
- How does my knowledge of grammar help me? E.g. *elle **a avalé** le bonbon*: I can tell that this is a verb in the past tense.
- Do the questions I have to answer help me to know what the text is about?

Speaking and writing:

- Can I make myself understood by pointing, gesturing, miming or drawing?
- Can I use a word which means almost the same thing?
- Can I get round a word I've forgotten by explaining or describing what I mean? E.g. ***Die Schwester meiner Mutter** wohnt in Hamburg.*
- Can I find an easier way to say the same thing? E.g. *Die Straße ist zu* instead of *Man hat die Straße gesperrt.*
- Are there general words I can use in case of difficulty? E.g. *chose, machin, truc, Ding, Dingsbums, cosa.*

 ## USING THE STRATEGIES

Obviously, pupils need to know not only what strategies are available: they also need practice in deciding which strategies are appropriate in which situation, as well as practice in applying them. In addition to doing specific practice activities, it is important to encourage pupils to use these strategies in the normal course of their work.

Here are some suggestions:

- ► Pupils go through a text scoring out words they don't know. They then read through the text and see how much they can still understand.
- ► As part of a reading activity, pupils have to pick out in the text the key words they need to know to carry it out. This highlights the number they **don't** need to understand.
- ► When pupils are doing a reading activity, you could display on the board or OHP a list of strategies to avoid overuse of the dictionary. The pupils have to think about these as they work through the activity and say afterwards which they found useful.
- ► When preparing or going over written or spoken work on a given topic, you could encourage pupils to think of alternative ways of saying particular things.

The above strategies will help to make pupils more self-reliant and competent in their use of the language, and reduce their dependence on the dictionary and on the teacher.

At the same time, on-going discussion regarding the situations in which pupils do **not** need to use a dictionary will also highlight how useful the dictionary is in other circumstances.

3. Using a dictionary in an exam

It is clear that using the dictionary effectively involves a considerable amount of skill and training, without which it can be as much of a hindrance as a help. This is also true regarding its use in exams. Pupils must be well prepared to take maximum advantage of their dictionary, and at the same time avoid misusing it.

It is important to stress to pupils the major issues:

- They should make good use of the dictionary — it is there to help them.
- However, since time in the exam is limited, use of the dictionary must be limited.
- Inappropriate use of the dictionary can lead to disaster!

To help them address these issues, pupils need to have strategies at their fingertips. Some are suggested below. Discuss with your pupils well in advance of the exam which ones they find most useful and give them plenty of opportunities to put these strategies into practice. Pupils also need to be fully aware of when dictionary use is allowed in the exams - this will vary from board to board (for example, in the listening exam, some boards allow dictionaries before and after pupils listen to the tape, while others do not allow dictionaries at all).

 ## HINTS & TIPS

Be familiar with your dictionary! Make sure you know how to use it properly and quickly. Practice makes perfect!	Suggestions for ways of learning to use the dictionary are outlined in Chapter 2. As well as being able to find words quickly, can they also find useful features such as verb tables and phrases for writing letters? Pupils will achieve real familiarity with the dictionary only by using it regularly throughout the course.
Look carefully at what you are asked to do in a reading question. You probably won't need to understand all the words in a text to be able to answer the question.	As pupils tackle reading questions in class or for homework, you can discuss with them which words and phrases they need to understand, and which are not needed for the task in hand.

Save time in a reading test by using the strategies you know to help you work out what words mean *without* using the dictionary.	Some useful strategies are described in Chapter 2.
Where possible, stick to words you already know when speaking and writing. Using the dictionary a lot will take too much time, and could also lead to unnecessary mistakes.	Encourage your pupils to do this by discussing with them alternatives to particular examples. You can easily build this in to the normal oral and written work you do in class.
Avoid wasting time in the speaking and writing tests by only looking up words and phrases which you will *definitely* need.	Pupils can sometimes be tempted to look up various alternatives in advance, for example in a writing exam. They need to learn to be disciplined, plan what they definitely want to say, and only look up a small number of vital words if this is unavoidable.
Be realistic about how many words you will have time to look up in the exam.	You could try the following experiment. Give pupils a list of sentences, each with a word underlined. How many of the words can pupils look up in five minutes? They might be surprised at how few this is. This should help them to be aware of how limited their dictionary use must be in an exam.
Don't use the dictionary for double-checking words you are fairly sure you know. You should only double-check if there is enough time at the end.	Conscientious pupils sometimes need to have more confidence in themselves. The pupils who prefer to double check are often the ones who were right first time round! They must not let their conscientiousness hinder them in the exam.
Plan how and when you will use your dictionary in the exam.	Discuss with pupils different strategies for making the best use of the limited time they have for using the dictionary. One strategy, for example, is to aim to answer all the questions as well as possible without the dictionary, leaving time at the end for dictionary work. Alternatively, they could limit themselves to essential dictionary use as they work through, and use any extra time at the end for extra checking. In any case, pupils need to be aware that pacing themselves as they work through an exam paper is an important skill in general.

4. Managing the dictionary

 ## THE SCHEME OF WORK

Since the National Curriculum and Scottish 5–14 Guidelines require pupils to be taught to use dictionaries and reference materials, any departmental scheme of work should have this skill explicitly built into it, however briefly, and in such a way as to show progression. While individual departments will decide for themselves how best to do this, the following suggestions could be borne in mind.

It would be a good starting point to liaise with the English department in your school, and discuss its policy and time-scale for the development of dictionary skills. The use of dictionaries also needs to dovetail with any reading scheme that your own department has in place.

The progression outlined in the National Curriculum level descriptions could usefully be borne in mind as you build dictionary skills into your Scheme of Work.

READING

- In the receptive skill of reading (AT3), the first mention of pre-dictionary skills is at Level 2, where pupils 'use books or glossaries to find out the meanings of new words'. This clear reference to glossaries and how to use the 'mini-dictionaries' which are at the backs of most coursebooks is a useful starting point to include in a Scheme of Work for the first year of a foreign language course.
- By Level 3, pupils are beginning to use a bilingual dictionary to look up new words.
- This is seen as an easier skill than 'using context to deduce the meaning of unfamiliar language' which comes at Level 4. The Scheme of Work should ensure that progression takes place, so that pupils do not come to over-rely either on you or on dictionaries.
- Beyond this level, dictionary skills are subsumed under 'reference materials', and your Scheme of Work for each year group should refer to this growing confidence, accuracy and autonomy of use.

WRITING

- The first mention of dictionary skills in the more active skill of writing (AT4) is at the later stage of Level 4. Here, learners 'are beginning to make appropriate use of dictionaries and glossaries as an aid to memory', and not for looking up previously unknown words.
- At Level 5, pupils are encouraged 'to look up unknown words', since their greater awareness of linguistic functions is such that they are more likely to make sensible use of the dictionary. The Scheme of Work should reflect this progression.
- At Levels 7 and 8, students are expected to make more autonomous use of reference sources and materials 'to extend their range of language and improve accuracy'.

FOR BOTH SKILL AREAS

- The Scheme of Work should reflect the specific needs of pupils using the dictionary under exam conditions at GCSE and Standard Grade.
- Dictionary skills, including monolingual, should be further developed post-16.

In planning dictionary skills within your Scheme of Work, you will need to address the following key issues:

- Progression of skills across the year groups.
- How to integrate development of these skills into the course, e.g. How much time and how often?
- Use of the target language or English.

It should be stressed in the Scheme of Work that dictionary skills need to be integrated carefully and consistently into normal lessons, and not seen as an occasional 'bolt-on' extra which is unrelated to normal work. Dictionary skills need to be learned as applied skills, and regular practice will have more impact than longer, but isolated, sessions.

 ## LEARNING FROM THE DICTIONARY

Clearly, even the most skilful dictionary use alone will not by itself increase pupils' vocabulary. They therefore need to be taught not just how to find words in a dictionary, but also how to sift, record and learn these words, so that they pass into pupils' active or at least passive vocabulary.

Because dictionary use is largely a private and individual process, pupils need to take charge themselves of the process of expanding their vocabulary. Human nature being what it is, there needs to be some encouragement and structure to this.

SIFTING

The first step in organising the new knowledge that a dictionary provides is to sift out unwanted items. Some words that a pupil looks up are not worth the effort of trying to remember. Activities to practise sifting could include the following:

- ▶ Give the class a list of nine words in the target language that include three very useful words for the stage they are at, three words of probable use and interest, and three words that are unlikely to be of use. Pupils have to look them all up, and to categorise them under these three headings, and then to compare their list with a neighbour and to discuss why they placed them where they did.
- ▶ Give the class a short passage in the target language from a reader, and ask pupils to underline with the aid of a dictionary five words that they think will be useful and five that they think will not be of use, and again to compare their ideas with each other giving reasons.
- ▶ Pupils note down words they thought were useful from their free reading, and test each other in pairs on what they have learnt. This has the advantage of allowing pupils to query why they chose to note certain words.

RECORDING

Having decided what words to make a note of, the next step is how to record them. Different schools and classes and pupils will decide for themselves, but points to consider might include:

- Should words be noted in a full size separate exercise book, at the back of the pupil's normal exercise book, in a small vocabulary notebook, or on loose leaves in a ring-binder?
- Should words be noted down in the random order in which they crop up in texts, or organised in some way, e.g. alphabetically, by function, by topic, or by synonyms?
- Should English be used at all when noting down vocabulary, or is some other way such as pictures or target language synonyms preferable?
- If English is used, should words be written down with the target language first and English second, or vice versa?
- Should pupils note down single words, or illustrative phrases with the words in context?

- Should words like nouns be noted with the definite article in front of them, or should gender be denoted with abbreviations like *m* or *f* after the noun?

Whatever system and method is chosen, it needs to be applied systematically, with time in class and homework devoted to it.

LEARNING

It cannot be stressed enough to pupils that learning is never something that happens by accident, but is something that must be done actively. *'C'est en forgeant qu'on devient forgeron.'* Pupils could try some of the following suggestions, and see if they can come up with some of their own.

- When pupils think they have learnt some new words for the topic they are studying, they write them out without any vowels. After doing some other homework or after dinner, they try to write them out in full by filling in the missing vowels. They then write the correct English meanings alongside.
- Pupils record on cassette a group of new words from a topic, leaving a gap between the target language and the English equivalent. They play the first part, pause the recording and try to say the English before letting the recording run on. The order could be reversed to hear the English first.
- Pupils write each word to be learnt on a different piece of paper, repeating it aloud as they do so. On the other side of the paper they draw a picture representing the word. They then try to say the new word just by looking at their drawings.
- Pupils write each word to be learnt on a piece of paper, and stick it up on their bedroom wall or by the toilet, so that they keep being reminded of them several times a day.
- If there are phrases or words in context to be learnt, pupils could copy a group of phrases onto a piece of paper, then blank out every other word. They do something else for a while, and then come back to the task and try to fill in the gaps.
- Pupils try to learn new words by a kind of word association game. For example, *piscine* might suggest *poisson*; *horloge* might suggest *heure*.
- Pupils could set themselves anagrams to solve the next day, e.g. the German for *castle* is *das ßlsohc*.
- Pupils write a set of several new words on separate pieces of paper. They shuffle the pieces of paper, face down, and remove one without looking at it. They turn over all the others and see if they can identify the missing phrase.

▶ Pupils copy out words or phrases in categories, according to their own preferences or habits, e.g. food they like / dislike; or in a specific order, e.g. sports from most to least favourite.

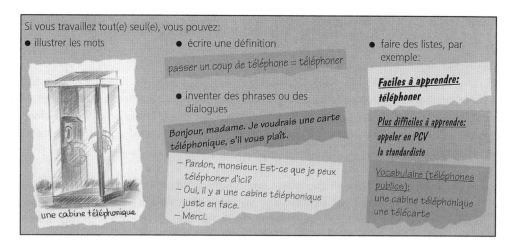

Si vous travaillez tout(e) seul(e), vous pouvez:

● illustrer les mots

une cabine téléphonique

● écrire une définition

passer un coup de téléphone = téléphoner

● inventer des phrases ou des dialogues

Bonjour, madame. Je voudrais une carte téléphonique, s'il vous plaît.

– Pardon, monsieur. Est-ce que je peux téléphoner d'ici?
– Oui, il y a une cabine téléphonique juste en face.
– Merci.

● faire des listes, par exemple:

Faciles à apprendre:
téléphoner

Plus difficiles à apprendre:
appeler en PCV
la standardiste

Vocabulaire (téléphones publics):
une cabine téléphonique
une télécarte

(Buckby and Berwick, *Auto Examen B*, Collins Educational)

5. Practical dictionary issues

 ## CHOOSING A DICTIONARY

Dictionaries range from the cheapest small pocket dictionary to more sophisticated and technical tomes. Before choosing a dictionary, the first requirement is to weigh up the issue of appropriateness for particular students against the finite departmental resources at your disposal.

Whether buying a set of one type of dictionary to suit a range of pupils, or a variety of dictionaries to suit particular needs, you will need to take a detailed look at the range on offer. The following guidelines outline some important criteria to bear in mind when selecting a bilingual or monolingual dictionary, and should help you make an informed and appropriate choice.

SELECTION CRITERIA

Three basic criteria for judging dictionaries have been identified by Sidney Landau in *Dictionaries. The art and craft of lexicography* (p306):

> **1** quantity of information
>
> **2** quality of information
>
> **3** effectiveness of presentation

1 quantity of information

- How many entries are there?
- How many definitions are there?
- How many new terms are in it compared to other dictionaries?
- How many idiomatic usages are there?
- Are synonyms given?
- Is there a guide to the pronunciation of words, and in what form?
- Are proper names and abbreviations included?
- Are there verb tables, ordinal/cardinal numbers, sections on telling the time, weights, measures, etc?
- Does it list useful phrases for writing letters, etc?

- How accurate are the entries?
- How complete is the information?
- How clear is the information?
- How up-to-date is the information?
- Are words cross-referenced, e.g. if you look up *suis*, will you be referred to *être*?
- Does the entry give helpful hints, e.g. whether a verb takes the dative or not?
- In what year was the dictionary brought out or last revised?

3   effectiveness of presentation

- Is the typography clearly legible?
- Are there too many columns of text on a page for ease of use?
- Is the section on how to use the dictionary clear?
- Is there a section of activities to show pupils how to use a dictionary?
- Are there any graphics or pictures?
- Is colour used to highlight headwords?
- Are parts of speech indications in English or the target language?
- Was it written with English learners of the target language in mind? For example, a dictionary written for French people might have a section on American versus English usages, which would be irrelevant for our pupils, or a dictionary written for German people might not give the plural form of German nouns. Conversely, some monolingual dictionaries are specifically written with the non-native learner in mind.

In short, will the layout help pupils to find what they want quickly and easily?

MAKING THE SELECTION

Clearly, you will need to decide which of the different aspects carry most importance for your own situation, because the ideal dictionary for an advanced student may be overwhelming for a beginner. It may be helpful to make your own short checklist of words appropriate to your pupils' needs, against which you could judge comparable dictionaries. For example, for younger pupils this list may include words such as *mountain bike*; *gerbil* and *computer games* and parts of common irregular verbs given as headwords, such as *suis*, while for advanced students, the list may include more technical words to do with contemporary issues, such as *ozone layer, subscription channel*, and terms to do with social issues, such as *single parent family* or *drug pushing*.

Money will obviously be a vital factor (particularly for some minority languages: see below), so as well as weighing up the above criteria against the initial cost implications, another practical issue to consider is whether the cover of the dictionary is hardwearing or washable, since a cheaper but flimsy edition may be a false economy in the long run.

 ## PROVISION

Neither SCAA nor the exam boards recommend any particular dictionary, nor do they provide any funds for the purchase of dictionaries. The comparison often drawn is with calculators: pupils are encouraged to buy their own, and schools are free to advise pupils on what they feel might be a good buy. Clearly, schools will need to have a stock of dictionaries available for exams for those pupils who either cannot or will not buy their own, or who fail to bring them to the exam on the day.

Many schools now send letters to parents of new pupils recommending a particular dictionary, and offering the facility to order it through the school at a reduced price. Here is a sample letter from one school, showing how parents are given information about dictionaries, tying them into the home reading scheme.

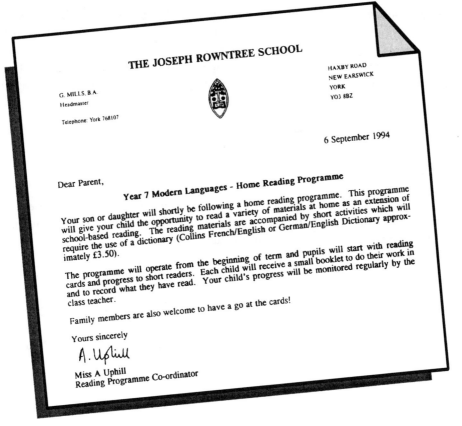

THE JOSEPH ROWNTREE SCHOOL

G. MILLS. B.A.
Headmaster

Telephone: York 768107

HAXBY ROAD
NEW EARSWICK
YORK
YO3 8BZ

6 September 1994

Dear Parent,

Year 7 Modern Languages - Home Reading Programme

Your son or daughter will shortly be following a home reading programme. This programme will give your child the opportunity to read a variety of materials at home as an extension of school-based reading. The reading materials are accompanied by short activities which will require the use of a dictionary (Collins French/English or German/English Dictionary approximately £3.50).

The programme will operate from the beginning of term and pupils will start with reading cards and progress to short readers. Each child will receive a small booklet to do their work in and to record what they have read. Your child's progress will be monitored regularly by the class teacher.

Family members are also welcome to have a go at the cards!

Yours sincerely

A. Uphill

Miss A Uphill
Reading Programme Co-ordinator

AVAILABILITY

A related issue is the cost of bilingual dictionaries for certain less commonly taught languages. Although dictionaries are available, they can be costly, and sometimes come in two volumes rather than the more convenient one. As an example, the Oxford Universal English-Gujarati dictionary costs £7.95. For this reason, some exam boards are willing to allow the use of glossaries rather than dictionaries in exams for some languages (but not for common European ones). This needs to be checked with your exam board.

There are other considerations for some schools. There are, for example, no large-print bilingual dictionaries for the visually impaired, nor are there any bilingual dictionaries French–Welsh Welsh–French for those learning French in Welsh-medium schools. In these cases, pupils could be disadvantaged in formal exams, where speed using a dictionary is a factor. It might well be worth contacting your exam board to find out what allowances can be made.

 ## ELECTRONIC DICTIONARIES

Electronic dictionaries can be bought for computers on floppy discs or CD-ROMs, and can be used in conjunction with a word-processing package. Students should be made aware of and encouraged to use any such software which you have in your school. Portable pocket translators are now available specifically for GCSE and the National Curriculum. Some of these even have an 'intelligent' close-match spell-correction facility. However, they are currently not permitted in exams.

 ## SCHOOL LIBRARY PROVISION

The role of the school library in encouraging dictionary use must not be forgotten. It is worth checking with the school librarian whether there might be some funding available for upgrading Modern Languages reference materials.

> *The school library should be seen as part of the MFL department's pool of resources, . . . for reading and reference materials and other resources.*
> (MFL Non-statutory guidance 1992 p.H6)

Pupils should be aware of the range of reference materials available in the library and where to find them.

Conclusion

If pupils have been taught how to use a dictionary effectively:

- they will become more competent language users;
- they will show improved attitude towards the subject;
- their self-esteem will increase, since they will be in a better position to solve problems for themselves rather than be too dependent on the teacher;
- they will be able to concentrate better on the task in hand.

If teachers know that a class can use a dictionary effectively:

- this is an aid to greater variety of teaching methods;
- this relieves the teacher of the need to be a walking dictionary;
- this lets teachers deal with more important problems than items of vocabulary.

Bibliography and references

Beattie N, 'Teaching dictionary use' in *Modern Languages*, vol LIV, No 4 (Dec. 1973)

Buckby M and G Berwick, *Auto Examen B* (Collins Educational, 1992–)

Buckby M and S Thorne, *Solo 2* (Collins Educational, 1994)

Carter R and M McCarthy, *Vocabulary and Language Teaching* (Longman, 1988)

Department for Education, *MFL in the National Curriculum* (DfEE, 1995)

Evans M, *Dictionary skills Spanish* (Language Centre Publications, 1995)

Horsfall P, *Dictionary skills French* (Language Centre Publications, 1995)

Horsfall P, *Dictionary skills German* (Language Centre Publications, 1995)

Landau S, *Dictionaries. The art and craft of lexicography* (CUP, 1989)

McCarthy M, *Vocabulary* (OUP)

NEAB, *GCSE Syllabus*

Pillette M, *Developing dictionary skills in French* (Collins Educational, 1996)

Scottish Office Education Department, *Modern European Languages 5–14* (SOED, 1991)

Strathclyde Regional Council, *Dictionary skills*

Tayside Regional Council, *Dictionary skills in the French class*

Thompson G, 'Using bilingual dictionaries' in *ELT Journal,* No 41 (1987)

Appendix: The dictionary in British schools

There are now clear guidelines regarding dictionary use in state schools in Scotland, England and Wales.

THE DICTIONARY IN THE CURRICULUM

The post-Dearing National Curriculum for England and Wales requires that: 'Pupils should be taught to use dictionaries and reference materials' (PoS Part 1; 3d).

As early as Level 2 in AT3 (Reading and Responding) pupils are expected to 'use books and glossaries to find out the meanings of new words', going on to use a bilingual dictionary or glossary at Level 3. At Level 5, they should be 'more confident in . . . their use of reference materials', and by Level 8, 'consult a range of reference materials as appropriate'.

First mention in AT4 (Writing) is made at Level 4: 'They are beginning to make appropriate use of dictionaries and glossaries as an aid to memory'. By Level 5, pupils should be using dictionaries or glossaries 'to look up unknown words'. From there, they use reference materials increasingly, for accuracy and variety of expression.

The Scottish 5–14 guidelines state that, as they are exposed to a greater quantity of reading material, pupils 'have to learn ways of helping themselves by use of word lists, glossaries, dictionaries'. In their reading, they are expected to 'make use of reference materials such as word lists, glossaries and dictionaries with increasing accuracy and independence'. Reference materials should also be available for guidance as required at Intermediate and Level E of the Writing AT.

THE DICTIONARY IN EXAMS

Use of dictionaries or glossaries is permitted in many components of the new GCSE and Standard Grade, A and AS level, Higher Grade and CSYS/Advanced Higher exams. Indeed, at the GCSE Higher Tier, the dictionary is particularly important now that there is no longer a wordlist for this tier. If they are not to be disadvantaged, therefore, all pupils need to be able to use a dictionary successfully.

Key Stage 3 assessment activities (whether your own or the non-statutory KS3 assessment materials from SCAA) will also often assume that pupils have access to dictionaries and reference materials.

In Northern Ireland, dictionary use is not at present permitted in public exams.